Trial By Ordeal

Trial By Ordeal

Poetry

KAREN MOBLEY

RESOURCE *Publications* • Eugene, Oregon

TRIAL BY ORDEAL
Poetry

Copyright © 2020 Karen Mobley. All rights reserved. Except for brief quotations in critical publications or reviews, no part of this book may be reproduced in any manner without prior written permission from the publisher. Write: Permissions, Wipf and Stock Publishers, 199 W. 8th Ave., Suite 3, Eugene, OR 97401.

Resource Publications
An Imprint of Wipf and Stock Publishers
199 W. 8th Ave., Suite 3
Eugene, OR 97401

www.wipfandstock.com

PAPERBACK ISBN: 978-1-7252-6900-2
HARDCOVER ISBN: 978-1-7252-6899-9
EBOOK ISBN: 978-1-7252-6901-9

Manufactured in the U.S.A. 05/01/20

Gimp Club was included in Try this at Home: An Anthology Chapbook from the Spokane's Diverse Voices Writing Group, 2019

For Mom, Dad, and Curt

Contents

Washing Feet | 1
Seen Enough? | 2
Fallen Rock | 4
My Father | 5
On Learning Mom Has Lou Gehrig's Disease | 7
Housing the Blue Bird | 8
Pain Management | 10
Topic of Cancer | 11
Ash after the Fire is Gone | 13
Heron | 14
The Door | 15
Order Astonishment | 16
Rabbits Tell the Saddest Tales | 18
Illustrations of Hell | 19
Learning to Turn | 20
Saintpaulia—In Praise of African Violets | 21
How We Understand the Believing | 23
Post-Operative Instructions | 25
Dancing to Two Musics—New Mexico, 1998 | 27
Cotton Tail Standing | 29
Drawing Darkness | 30
Doubting | 31
Gimp Club | 32
Lithopedion: Stone Child | 34
On the One Hand, on the Other Hand | 35
Pretending to Catch | 36
Stubborn | 37
Missing Fingers | 38

Seldom Seen | 39
Question: Why Don't You Put Me Down? | 40
Names That I Do Not Know | 42
Occupied | 45
In the Wind | 46
How It Comes Back | 48
Two-Star Day | 50
The Day Was Found | 51
Love in a Drawer | 53
Ruby Throat and the Sword Swallower: A True Story | 54
After a House a'Fire | 55
Don't Throw That Letter Away—It Contains My Only Original Thought. | 57

WASHING FEET

> Stood at his feet, him weeping,
> began to wash his feet with tears
> wipe them with the hairs of her head
> kissed and anointed his feet
> with ointment.
>
> —Luke 7:38

I see your face with its tears
sadness stuck in your throat.
The earthquake that is you, Mom
speaks the language it knows
weeping.

There is nothing to do but wash *feet,*
your black toes, sores, painful peeling skin
in cool water. I washed your feet. Your skin came off.

I hide my tears and kiss you, hold you close.
You *forgive me.*

I know that you will never move again, hike
with your Audubon book and binoculars.
You will never dance or comb your hair.
You are trapped in your body like gnats
stuck in *an ointment.*

Under my skin, rage seethes.
The whole world is broken, waiting
for the call that will tell us
you have left our world
the earthquake
taking your birds
your sight
your pain.

SEEN ENOUGH?

Death is never a single end
but a collection of ends...so tightly bound together they appear as one.

                    UNKNOWN

I.

I look up into yellow gopher teeth of grief.
I need to see. I want to hide.
Perhaps, I could ask you to lash
my eyes open so that I can see fully
columbines and blue flax
not poppies with their flaming petals. Purple
lilacs and old-fashioned roses make tears flow.

Mom used to say, "seen enough?"
When she had studied detail of bird with her binoculars,
she'd lower her head and her voice. *Seen enough?*

She took pictures of every place. We'd sit quietly
look at photos of Arizona or the Mississippi River.
She'd say, "seen enough?" and go to fix dinner.

II.

One visit, for three identical days—
breakfast at eight o'clock, pills, dishes
a drive down Beach Loop.

Dad goes for coffee. I sit still.
Wait for her.
I bake pumpkin pie
scrub the kitchen, clean the refrigerator,
wash dishes, fold and comfort the laundry
hear dogs bark
listen to country music,
look across at the neighbor's house.

She says, "I'm a nuisance."
"This disease is changing my nature."
Truer words were never said.
Her nature was warm, kittens in sun
sweet as bourbon and seven.

She is ready to be driven down the coast,
to another pullout to look out the
car window at waves. Sanderlings and gulls. Seen Enough?

III.

She is like sea lion on rock,
sedentary, she can't move her head.
She has seen enough miserable
old rain, the terrible old man of grey.
She has seen enough.

IV.

I've not seen enough. Not enough
of heart shaped aspen leaves
or small blue butterflies.
or the goldfinch,
thunderclouds
or swallows.
See them
fly over our heads.

FALLEN ROCK

We drive sixty miles to Gold Beach.

My mother owns this beach, rubs it like you rub your foot.
She massages with her mind, every rock, tide pool,
each spot where a sea anemone might hide.
She recites the site of elk, deer, sanderling,
goose gull, cormorant. She knows the roads, the paths.
She can't walk but directs me where to walk on her behalf.

My mother owns these birds like you own the skin on your palm.
She knows fox sparrows, white crown, varied thrush,
towhee, pygmy nuthatch, flickers. Mom is an agate found on the beach
worn down, edges roughed off, worn—with perfectly manicured hands,
long nails from doing nothing—no dishes, no garden, no motion.
She is worn from moving her mind, her heart, her grief.

My father sits in the back seat, eyes closed.
He has been with her since forever. Together, since before he tied her shoes
before lift chair, before walker, before commode, before wheelchair.
He remembers her like she remembers this beach. He fills her
with life by reminding everyone who she was, what she
did, what she said when she could.

The sign says to watch for falling rock—right here on the line, the yellow line
beside the road. The language that is moving, that is walking, is deafness.
Her body is dumb, unspeaking. The language that is her body is stuttering,
gasping as walking goes away. Here her mind slips in and out of the present.
Her voice pulls in and out of sorrow. Her jaws don't work.
Swallowing begins to fail. She cannot bring a glass to her mouth.

She is a fallen rock slipping to the beach and into the sea.

MY FATHER

For David Mobley

His blue eyes are sharp. He drives along in the truck
slows down, points into a field, a baby antelope
standing so still it is barely there. He'll get out a spotting
scope or binoculars. Point. Set your eye on the nest.

When I was young, he was so tall I could barely see
the blue of his eyes when he was standing.
He would hold his finger down, I would wrap my hand,
full palm, against his finger and we would walk.
We would walk toward the horse pasture, down by the swing,
near the horseradish plant. He would place the saddle pad,
lift me up onto a horse named Babe and I would ride in circles.
Later, I rode beside him. He rode Ab and I rode a horse
named Scooter on a small leather saddle.

When he had been busy, had not seen me for several days,
He'd come into the bedroom to wake me up to say hello.
I remember sitting on his lap, my head against his chest
listening to his breath and his heart as he scratched my back.
Sometimes, I would sit on his lap and he would draw witches,
guys with big ears and talk to me, only me there on his lap.

There at Sunlight Creek, he wore his waders and carried me
on his back, fishing poles in hand, my head over his shoulder,
soggy tennis shoes dripping down. He'd say *lean forward,
lean forward* and move with me so I don't fall on the rocks.
Don't fall on the rocks. He showed how to cast with spinner and fly.

My father loves cats. I think he always has. When I was small,
he showed me how to make the cat purr by pushing my
face against the warm fur on her belly, *brr brrrr brr* with my lips.

It is a beautiful creaking screen-door morning.
Cottonwood trees . . . Four herons in the rookery.
Six nests in the tree. Wings are blue grey,
heads white with black stripe. He points out the nest to me.
I think, if we could climb to the stick nests, we would find 3 to 7 eggs
the blue of my father's eyes.

ON LEARNING MOM HAS LOU GEHRIG'S DISEASE

Mom soon will sit still
like a still-life painting.
She puts apricots and cream
in a bowl and eats slowly,
chewing carefully while she can.
Soon she will sit in a chair
not moving but her mind will buzz
buzz like bees in the apricot trees.
Still life.
Still live.
Still eyes.

HOUSING THE BLUE BIRD

I want to help but there is nothing to do.

I.

I wake up when Dad leaves
in his loud diesel truck to drink coffee
with men from town. He goes out to see daylight.
Daylight is still there. I can see her
with her finches, robins, and towhees.
Sometimes she brings her doves.
They carry the light gently to the ocean.
I make coffee in an old percolator
and wait for Mom.

II.

Mom can't go out by herself now.
She doesn't feel confident, she falls
can't get up. She can't sew
feathers on birds
buttons on children's coats
or put the backs on the earrings.
She doesn't cry or weep.
Sometimes sadness gets out
gently tearing at the corner of her eye
or making a sad frail sound.
She tries to hide the awfulness
but she fails. With help, she walks
to the bench so she can see the sea
lions and feel the wind on her face
watch the waves. This wave
grabbed her hard and is pulling her in.

III.

My father loves my mother. I know.
I hear it in the way he says her name,
says *your mother*. As long as I remember,
he has always loved her. I know he will
stay with her even though there is nothing
to do but wait for her to stop breathing.
He takes her to the beach and for drives,
looks out, sees what she sees
able to tell small
brown bird from small brown bird
sparrow from sparrow
bluebird Eastern from Western.

IV.

Before I leave, I dream I am on a porch.
It smells like the softness of babies' feet.
I hear laughter like in a smoky bar with
men handsome as my father years ago.
It is as beautiful as Thomas Moran's
Grand Canyon of the Yellowstone.
When mothers die, they go there before
we build houses for them with tiny holes
for doors one and 6/8 inches around and
they come in away from sparrows
and starlings.

V

No woman was closer to daylight.
No woman was closer to Dad.
No woman is closer to a blue bird.
No woman was closer to a saint.
If there was ever one.

PAIN MANAGEMENT

Globes sit. Do not rotate.

Dad waits. I wait. We wait.

At his house, sunflowers,
in the side yard beam.

Later, amaryllis on a table tilts toward the sun.

We wait and lean
deep into the shadow
of the valley—you know the valley, I mean.
We look over and cannot see the bottom.

The doctor's say,

they can do nothing

not today, not tomorrow, not any day.

TOPIC OF CANCER

We need routine. There is nothing to still
the change, the slow diminishment. I seek
comforting noises of the house
television in another room, fire crackling,
fan moving, the gentle snuffling of an old cat
sleeping, the squeak of a door, to mask the sighing.

We do nothing.
We watch weight loss,
malnutrition and become

malcontented

develop a malaise.

Cancer is a sign
of the zodiac.

Mom was a Cancer.

My brother, Curt, was a Cancer.

Their deaths are a cancer
climbing Dad's esophagus like
pole beans on a stake.

Form tunnels and wells—darkness
deep shadows, not heaven
but deep space.

Coda—Codeine—Hydrocodone—Oxycodone
They say this is palliative care. It does not
sooth or placate or stop the pall a falling.
Ends with a crescendo.

We stay up all night together. Nice cabin you have here.
Dad says he will feel better when we get to a lower altitude.
He says we are walking. The trip has been long.
Will they speak English when we get there?

All night. The stories, the altitude, the nice cabin
you got here, do these people speak English?
When are we going to get there?
When are we going to get there?
Did you bring the beer?

I go with him until someone comes to meet him.

ASH AFTER THE FIRE IS GONE

Tuesday's sadness is silence in the room.

Tuesday's sadness is changing locks, throwing things away.

Tuesday's sadness is Negro Modelo.

Tuesday's sadness is Earl Grey.

Tuesday's sadness is orange seeds on mountain ash.

Tuesday's sadness is enchiladas.

No one will buy me a Christmas present.

I will chase a big cloud through the sky, stand like a crow
on a table and grow like an old-fashioned yellow rose bush in Wyoming sun.

Tuesday's sadness is bourbon and seven.

Tuesday's sadness is a tree with insistence on being green.

Tuesday's sadness is a man with globes, earths of many sizes silent and still
    on a shelf.

Tuesday's sadness is the icy edge of the creek.

Tuesday's sadness is having no one to call who will answer the phone.

Tuesday's sadness is the day after the day a year after my father died.

It is hard to run in this coat.

HERON

Sky reflects blues
Blue heron's feathers
Dad's blue eyes
fading to grey
to white with sadness.
Nests are high in the trees –
the trees with high dry branches.
The nests will fall when the tree does die.
She will lose her nest. Babies will cry.
He stands in the water up to his knee
with just one leg.

THE DOOR

There is the door.

A green door with a spotted curtain, a blue door frame,
singing of iris, sunflowers, and mountains.

The green door with a curtain echoes peacocks.
The door is hello.
The door is green with a yellow curtain.

What if outside the door there was a red geranium?
Or lonely Mexican woman holding a broom?

What if we stayed inside counting our money—
door closed—a dollar at a time?
Or we stayed inside because outside dogs bark?

There is a woman inside with an uneaten apple,
next to the door to the unseen, the unbidden, the unplanned.

ORDER ASTONISHMENT

I.

It's Lent. Forty days of pain.
Forty days on the respirator.
Forty days of waiting to die.
Forty days of waiting for the sun to shine.
Forty days of introspection.

Repent. Tramp all over like Christ.
Look for yourself. There is urgency.
Jesus was in a hurry. There is a whole world
out there—a big gut of geography.

II.

Surprise is a staple of life, like flour,
milk, eggs, lentils, split peas and grace.

Surprise is a small indulgence like cream in your coffee.
Sometimes evaporated milk in a can.

III.

I sit at a table with a red and black
oil cloth on the table, there is a big ceramic cup,
evaporated milk, a wooden chair,
frying eggs in a cast iron skillet,
a small boy with brown hair is drawing
on typing paper with a pencil
sharpened with a pocketknife.
He erases with a wet end of a finger.
He is a pretender. I am a pretender.

IV.

I am the girl with a ball cap,
an old fishing creel, a notebook and pencils,
pretending to be an artist,
I try to understand everything.

I struggle with my hands,
the low moon, Venus, comets, and the sun.

V.

Are we holding up?
Are we holding each other?
Are we holding on to the sky?
Do we cherish the sadness?
Are we holding on to the faithful dog of grief?
Are we holding this choir of sun
choir of rain?

What if Jesus was a comet, butterfly or robin?
What if our only reason for being is astonishment
with a side of salt and honey?

RABBITS TELL THE SADDEST TALES

when grasses dry and all is snow fall.
They still their ears, catch the echo
our dead travelling in wind.
They hold prayer with dew claw,
pain up into the weak spring sun.

Faithful, fertile, holding doubt,
failure on equal footing with birth
and death, finding food and footing
in dark snow and waiting for the spring
resurrection. Savior, small grass and crocus.

ILLUSTRATIONS OF HELL

Could I give up color for Lent?
Yellow's hot flash of holy spirit,
daffodils, sunflowers. Could I give up
the injured and dying,
the blood of crucifixion?
Could I give up green?
fresh lettuce or the smallest green
tinge on the top of the hill?
The purple, the lilacs, the horrible
stuffed dinosaurs, Job's daughters
old ladies' hats.

Could I give up science or enumeration?
The periodic table, the liturgical calendar,
an alphabetical list of names . . . Linnaeus named,
trying to capture mystery,
to cook and create blue, cobalt sulfite,
the sparkles from the wings of butterflies and dragon flies
and the feet of blue footed boobies.

Does giving up prove that God is real?
I think about sin, the aimlessness,
the pointlessness, drifting, giving up.

LEARNING TO TURN

With a nod to Matthew 5

At the Seattle Aquarium,
a blind rock fish learns to turn
his head to see. The veterinarian
gave him anesthesia, inserted a prosthetic
yellow glass eye. He needed
an eye, not to see. He is still blind.
He was bullied, picked on by fish, bigger,
stronger, sullied, prodded, poked.
He avoided his tank mates.
He has learned to turn.

The turned cheek,
the looking away,
the not
acknowledging
or noticed.

He turns and turns.
He can see, can't see.
They leave him be.

SAINTPAULIA—IN PRAISE OF AFRICAN VIOLETS

After Walter von Saint Paul—Illaires

I.

It's Sunday. Instead of church, I read poems, stories of saints, and ponder
   St. Paul.
Not Minnesota or the Apostle, but an African violet—Saintpaulia.
This lustful, irreverent plant blooming, beams as if resurrected
here in the low morning light of our dining room.

The Apostle was beheaded in the year sixty-seven after a second imprison-
   ment by the Romans.
The violet deadheaded in August, begins to bloom again.

II.

I desire more than green and purple cabbage in morning frost.
I desire more than delicate hollyhock seed pods in frozen shine.
I desire more than low sun blaring in west windows.
I desire more than the raw ambition of my immigrant heritage.
I desire more than the need, to survive not die.
I desire the strength to live on a rocky face in the cloud forest of Africa
like this saint—Saintpaulia.

III.

I am in awe of hummingbird's torpor state.
I am in awe of galaxies, endless space.
I am in awe of bacteria, its ability to destroy.
I am in awe of tenacity.
I am in awe of neurological systems, chi,
life force, electricity, tall tales told to muscles by our brains.
I am in awe of frost. Look, carefully, it is beautiful.
Walk delicately, you might fall.
I am in awe of fire,
its ability to lure cats into a seductive trance.
I am in awe of skin, a coating of cells that protects us,
a farm of microscopic life. I am in awe of glass,
sand made solid. I am in awe of apples and pears.

I am in awe of onions' power to heal
the many layers of shedding skin.
I am in awe of this Saintpaulia
that grows as if all life depended upon it

HOW WE UNDERSTAND THE BELIEVING

For the Mother Teresa and all the doubters

The sun shall be turned to darkness and the moon to blood (Acts 1—27)

Don't quit right before the miracle.
Stare into the blue vault of the sky.
Be thankful for the moon.

Don't be blind to the miracle.
Hear the loon across the lake.
Bring voice to the asking.

Old lady's prayers
heard from two blocks away.
They voice not a thing.

Kingfisher stands
balanced on a branch.
The tiny, tiny toad swims

in the river.
The kingfisher rattles
asking for fish to show themselves

so that he may be fed.
Have faith in the green clearing
in the trees and the true blue of the sky.

Stay put.
A big bowl of peaches
rests quietly in forgiveness.

Do something small.
Do not ask for too little.
Ask. Then listen carefully.

Don't be blind. You will find lost objects.
What is blind? Believe in the blue birds.
Believe the change.

A path lined carefully
with small rocks, magenta of wild geranium.
God created the infinite silence

in which we could be born.
Tri—color heron.
He is fishing.

His neck in perfect curve
complete with perfect tension
waiting for the bugs to skim

toward him,
a perfect reflection
in the sun.

POST-OPERATIVE INSTRUCTIONS

For J.P.

Seduce me with letters written on parchment,
in sealed envelopes, signed With Love.
Wake me with aromatic coffee in a ceramic mug
black, sugar, strong with cream. Comfort me
with uninterrupted sleep, not drugged like this
after surgery, like at the beach.
Long, lazy, loving at daylight—awakening golden
I like you in person—raw and present. Not like this,
on the phone. But when I can smell, taste, touch tongue.
You. You.

They said, do not make important personal or
business decisions for 24 hours. I love you. I decided.
Do not drive or operate machinery. I want you. I drive.
I fly with you to Italy, Umbria, see Piero della Francesca.
Ice for 20 minutes every two hours. Weight bearing
as tolerated. I bear your love.

You call, tell me that you are painting
your house burnt sienna, berry, pretending Tuscany.
I think about painting my house. I look down at my toes
colored iodine and red with the crusted blood.
You check on me. I still love you. I love your golden
light, your blue mountains. I want to climb you
like wisteria, touch your dimples with my thumbs.

On Sunday, you will go to the beach with your lover.
On Sunday, I will change bandages—stand longer.

Orthopedic instructions. They say not to turn my ankle.
I might not walk again. Tear the stitches. I say, don't tell.
I might wreck it. Tear us apart.

I never speak of you. You are secret. The unspoken.
The private. The held tight against my skin, like scapula
under clothing. I taste you—musky red wine
sun, hot flesh in desert, dust to fresh laundered shirts
adobe buildings, blue doorways, snakeskin boots
sun, ginger and chili. Red. Gold. Quiet meetings
in afternoons and when traveling—
unaided, unguided, unrestrained.

You walk the beach. Seagulls bathe, waves
crash, you gather daisies, red gladiolas,
arrange in the living room. You carefully select
red wine, golden cheese, windows facing west.
I try to straighten it out—alphabetical order, color, size
shape, walking from room to room balancing
carefully
on my foot.

My solitude sits on a table
its surface inscribed with stories
of children I will never know.
I heat up slowly like yeast bread rising.
I take for granted the palm tree of your affection.
The richness of your voice, the soft hair of your back.
There is a constant motion on the beach. Through small
gestures I recognize your mood.
You are gone but your smell stays with me.

Weight bearing as tolerated. I cannot bear the weight
of this unexpressed love any longer. I want
a letter, coffee, a night where I sleep beside you,
a day where we see mountain, smell sage and cilantro,
sit by the fire, golden, berry, blood. Tell me again
that when you can't sleep you think of my beautiful ankle
my delicate, tiny feet.

DANCING TO TWO MUSICS—NEW MEXICO, 1998

I.

I have New Mexico under my fingernails like dirt from the garden.
I smell it rich, fragrant and earthy. Its light is in my hair.
Its clouds float through the blue vault of my mind.
Your voice echoes in the canyon of the past.

II.

I go to you with finches in a cage and beer in a bottle.
I was an apprentice, grinding gristle of the heart,
Feeding you love without prudence.

III.

I hold onto my name with my teeth.
Birds hold their wings out to brush my face
softly and to hold your yes toward my
hands buried in the flesh of my chest.

IV.

The house is failing under the strain,
the buttresses, cracking of plaster,
notice the rain. I remember the delicate red tulip
of your glans, the seal shaped mole on your back, the delicate flicker
on the tree of your tongue. I waited for the silence of your
hands to end. I grasped tightly.

V.

Your eyes. You end the conversation
abruptly, clinch my face in your hand, pull on my face.
I hear a wailing hallow behind me.
Tape your milagro to your hand, I say
recognizing the furrow of your sorrow.

VI.

I sit still. I watch as she very carefully stitches
the tiny cross stitches into my heart. She counts
meticulously the veins, in, out and in,
then a few chain stitches from my heart to yours are
snipped. She cuts them quickly with sharp scissors, making sure
the pain will not go on. These stitches
make pictures-flowers and tears.

VII.

A flock of yellow-headed blackbirds light in the willows.
I dance two musics—to the tune of your loving
the melody of my leaving. You want to touch me.
You're a pretty little girl. I crave to touch
but try to miss the edges of my lust.

VIII

I close the drawer with the lock of hair.
Put it away.

IX.

I will not love someone who cannot gentle his voice.
You are too drunk to talk. Gentle your voice.
Put it softly on the table in front of you.

COTTON TAIL STANDING

on wind shifting sand
stretches up, pulls a branch
down to her mouth, bites,
chews, munches, devours
small leaves on branch.
I am a rabbit reaching.

DRAWING DARKNESS

Charcoal. Night drawing on paper.
A burned stick. Compressed trees.
Ground with dust. Dust without grit.
A puff tracked room to room, a cloud,
storm and another storm. Loud, clap, kick.
A fire, first of season, flames
lilac, tamarack, pine. Line, licks of fire
running through darkness.

DOUBTING

I.

The animal scientist on the radio warns us
of attributing too much to our pets
by anthropomorphizing behavior.
Mary, the cat, climbs up on me and purrs.
I doubt the man, not the cat.

II.

Soon it will be time to put up the Christmas tree.
Last year at this time, my father was dying,
we were sitting in this very room, as he was losing consciousness.
When I saw Dad dead, I knew was not coming back.
I saw him take his last breath. I know he is gone. I do not doubt.

III.

When I see you drive away, down the road
it is not always clear if you are leaving me,
when you will return, if you are late or befallen?
Where are you? Are you down the wash?
Across the sand dune? Gone to find the Xantus hummingbird,
a sun-faded robin or to buy a cup of coffee?

You are never clear, never explain, rarely commit.
I am left waiting, wondering, watching the hawks and vultures
soar overhead, waiting for the sun to go down, watching for you,
when do I start to look for you?
If you are broken, how will I pick you up?
I doubt that I will know.

GIMP CLUB

There are 27
bones in my right hand.
Nineteen in my left.
Symbrachydactyly.
Yes, this is the name of this
disorder.

In the Gimp Club,
all of us are
missing
bones
fingers
a hand or
hands
some
prehensile strength
the thumb that opposes
legs
leg
foot
toe
eye
or
a part of our mind.

There are 13
islands in the Galapagos
13 beans in the soup
Some people have 13 fingers
three extra, for no
discernable reason.
Polysyndactlyly.
Extra digits.

One in a hundred people are born
wrong or broken. Others get
broken along the way.

We are drunks mostly.
That is what we do together,
drink. We drink
dismiss
release
provide absolution.

We carry burdens
on hearts
that cannot be held
in our grasp.
We'd clasp hands
with you
but cannot.
We'd clap
enthusiastically
if you
performed
but we know
the sound
of the one hand
clapping.

LITHOPEDION: STONE CHILD

In one of every 11,000 pregnancies
a stone child—lithopedion—is formed.
A stone child weights inside mother's body for
forty years, dead but haunting, until mother
dies or has her child surgically removed.
Of all babies born alive, one is the Christ.

As I walk, I hear the water breaking against
rocks. I smell ocean, see shells calcified.
I feel stones in the road, smalled to gravel,
pushed aside. Stones. Rain. I feel the fallopian
pulled to ovary.

At the annunciation, the angel appears.
Promise—the birth calcified—angel appears.
Says, I will give birth. I refuse.
I create a stone baby.
Trapped inside for 43 years,
never being born, wrapped in a crust
like the ocean floor
to the southwest of my ovaries
born today with a knife wielded by
a surgeon looking for shipwrecks.
At the renunciation, the lithopedion is found.
Surrender is declared. Hummingbirds fly all night.
Sacrifice is given. We open our throats to blue sky.

The planet keeps its rhythm
even though my baby is trapped.
My stone child is dead but holds a laughter.
It can be broken free by thrown rocks.

It's Advent. Open your throat.
Throw your rock. Break your own water.

ON THE ONE HAND, ON THE OTHER HAND

I want to get on the horse
without my dad's help.
I cannot hold on to the saddle horn.
Born with short fingers on one hand,
I try to get up by standing on the bottom
fence wire. I want to be a trick rider
baton twirler and a dancer.

Now I pretend I am in the horse pasture
spinning in circles. I am alone
but I can hear my dad dropping his keys, change,
and pocketknife into a jar on the nightstand
as he readies for bed. Like cottonwood
I stand with proud anguish, my blood unspooling
as vermillion thread, bleeding as I did when I missed
the horse and fell into barbed wire.

PRETENDING TO CATCH

The boy hands me a ball.
Throw it, he says. Not like a girl.
Overhand, I think. I fling it slow.
I don't know how, girl or no girl.
No one taught me to throw because
of the second part, catching.
Dad steps in front of me stopping
the ball HARD as the boy throws it
back. Dad knows. I know.
When anything hits the ends
of my fingers, it burns all the way
to my shoulders, breaks the tiny bones,
makes me yearn to die. I fall. Stubborn.
I throw again, and again. Letting the ball
drop, never catching at all.

STUBBORN

Born with nubs for fingers, I chew
the fingers off my doll so her hand looks like mine.
I grow, know it is true. I am stubborn.
I think it is because my hand
is stubs, nubs. But not because of the nubs.
I won't turn away from the sun. I face into it
like a sunflower squinting into the unknown.

MISSING FINGERS

On the garage workbench a big box of nails
sharp and galvanized, big heads for kids to hit.
Pine board in the vice so we can pound, pound,
pound, pound. Nail after nail. Bent into the board,
bent, straighten, bent over and over, straight,
not bent, hammer in hand. I choke up
on the handle grab tightly, grab, slam, hit,
miss, bend, try again. I can smell metal,
pine, sweat, motor oil from the dripping
Pontiac, a sweet smell, Mom's sweet peas,
cars going by on the highway. I hear the sniffle of horse
stamping of hooves, tails snapping at flies.

I know all too soon I am never going to be
a carpenter or a boy. I learn to pound. Miss my fingers.

SELDOM SEEN

This poem requires a guitar, three rolls of wire,
two strangely shaped rocks, a well-crafted wooden
boat on a trailer, boat license 5238a, a yellow extension cord
with table saw attached, a garden wall, long handled tools,
a hoe, a watering can, a chicken fryer, a cast iron teapot,
a flexible flyer, a pear, a brown GMC pick-up, two of stacks of shingles
all begging to enter along with sawhorses, clothes that snap on a line,
a folding chair by the back fence, robins picking at a garden—worms,
arugula, onions, beets, tomato, a gate—*close the gate, keep the deer out
of the garden*—in the middle of town. Walking in the rain, I saw these things
and three bucks in velvet on the neighbor's lawn. The deer are gone
this morning. I sit in the garden, sitting so still that the squirrels
and ants walk across my feet as if my feet are rocks.
You, a too-thin stern-faced carpenter, seldom seen,
you beg to be in this poem, to lie like a deer under a tree,
to know my love, for you are my love, this is your garden.

QUESTION: WHY DON'T YOU PUT ME DOWN?

Toddlers, the aged, and wrong

I was born wrong. They held me too tight,
instilled in me curiosity, incessant questioning and bitching,
I'm always asking the wrong question.

Why will you not put me down?
Toddlers want down.
Do you see ghosts under the bed?

What companions are on your tricycle?
Why has the crime rate dropped since 1974?
What animals can swallow their selves? Whole or in pieces?

Does life have a better plan for you, if so, why are you so stupid?
Why don't they put you down?
Can you draw witches, cats or God?

Only when I see them, I say.
What do you want to do that actually earns money?
Do you know how many hands God has?

How do people learn to be good kissers
as opposed the ones who make you nervous
like they might swallow your entire human head?

Did you throw away my Barbies?
How is your libido?
Why will you not put me down?

What haunts you?
Why do cats have no hair? Why do we not put them down?
Why do crowns make such poetic sense when they are so uncomfortable?

What were you thinking about when I was born?
Where is the gateway to the sky?
What is the state tree?

Why do the states have birds?
Whatever happened to Jimmy Hoffa?
Who gives us permission?

Where do you go when you die?
What is the cat's last name?
How does God make snow?

Why is a penis shaped like that?
When do babies realize that they are people?
Where is the toilet?

What's for supper?
What is your middle name?
Do you have a saint's name?

What is the stopping place?
What the hell does corn starch do?
How do you know it is the correct answer?

So, he slides past me and says, "Is there enough miracle
to mold life into the vision of a pregnant God?"
You are no Stephen Hawking.

No kidding, I am no Stephen Hawking.
Why will you not put me down?
When you are dead, are you dead?

NAMES THAT I DO NOT KNOW

In Oaxaca, Mexico

I.

I call to the forest.

I listen

for the redheaded

Hungarian,

Romanian, dark haired and olive skinned,

Mexican

gorgeous bread of the universe

Gamboge of the sky

late night on television scary movie

the rattling song sparrow

A sore mosquito bite

A scrambled egg

A story untold.

II.

I hear the microscopic sound of butterflies

gently placing tiny feet on flowers,

moths gently striking light bulbs,

a hotel maid washing under the potted plant with a rag mop.

The chicken sounds. Roosters crow.

The old ladies talk down the hill.

Sadness sits on the windowsill.

Why do I feel better when flowers are red and

floors are turquoise?

III.
My imagination is strapped

like a man hauling a load of copper pipe.

I feel like a deaf person,

I ask for people to write

because I can read.

There is nothing coming

to me.

IV.
I smell bananas sweet smelling trees

sour skin without a shower

dusty desert before the rain.

It is a big valley below filled with

echo of dog barking and purple colored trees—

Jacaranda—a name I know.

Caracara, blue mockingbirds,

copal, bromeliad and cactus

cochineal.

Weavers weaving.

a flower lined nest—

Weaving, warp and weft,

the eye of water,

the god's eye

carding, spinning,

round bases and shapes

Not perfect but certain.

A man running down the road

with a wheelbarrow and the remnants of fire

to cook a small supper and to mark a trail

two dead dogs and one that is alive

unspeaking, me knowing

all I need to know

OCCUPIED

Despair is a toy with which we toggle.

Sit in your empty chair. Place your chair by the stream.
Place your chair in the field. Climb the ladder straight up
up into the sky.
Straight up,
straight backed,
straight forward,
straight and narrow,
strait or channel,
narrowing of the throat.
rushing anger stop.

Hold in the grip of teeth
Hide in folds of forgiveness
Clutch in the pockets of grief
the most important day.

A small dog watches the pelican fly,
Swirl, churl in circles and land
effortlessly in the stream. Still
four vultures sour the sky.

I am wounded—cracked, dry, like firewood.

Darkness is a state of being hard to see.
I am not wearing my glasses.
What do eyes prevent us from seeing?

I never studied a map that prepared me for the terrain underfoot.
The future is a difficult loss to accept.

IN THE WIND

With a nod to Acts 2

I kept walking down the street.
The giant rain from the humming
bird feeder dumped sugar water over me
made me sticky, bees began to swarm
ants came in the night, packing boxes came
with the scents of other cats,
dogs began to spray.

Again, and again the air thrusts
us to the ground in a big wind.

I began to read, words flew from the page
grabbed me by the hair, pulled,
as they were pulling, they became a swarm
of angry monkeys. "Your turn, your turn,"
Satan says, "It is your turn."
God says, "Seen enough?"
The monkeys held me down, pulled my ears and nose.

Thrust to the ground in a big wind.

My head was stuffed, my head was sore
a skunk slept in my car, mice formed
a nest. The cat is out, it wants back in,
when the cats is in and it wants out again.
I want God.
Who is God?
Gulls fly edge to edge.

Again, and again the air thrusts
us to the ground in a big wind.

My wings have melted
caught fire and I have fallen,
scratched myself with a pad for cleaning pots.
I attempt to reattach the limbs
and sew the eyes back into corpses.
Watch as if a sparrow in the rafters.

The big wind.

HOW IT COMES BACK

Down the street, I see three trees.
Nicely pruned trees with tiny oncoming leaves
green as tiny feathers on the head of a parrot,
tiny green leaves, I love but I do not love
the musty smell of the leaves where I hid
in your yard under the trees away from him.
Heart beating hard, pounding harder,
my chest aches. I breathe as if I am going
to faint dead, gasping, putting my hand over
my own mouth so I can still my breath.

I fall onto the ground, rest in the street, sweat.
I cannot run away. My legs fail, weak, frail.
Heart palpitating. Hands quivering.
Death, standing beside a pillar
under the underpass, screaming.
I wait for him to grab me by my collar or throw
a string around my neck, grab my hair, push me
nto an alley, rub my face in dog shit, grind my nose
against the wall and take me from behind It smells
like stale motor oil, garbage

burning, the stink of bourbon and unwashed hair.
He smells like my college boyfriend's aftershave.
Instead of grabbing me by the hair, he shows me his
crooked teeth. He apologizes. His eyes sparkle as if it is safe.
All in the head, my head is black from holding my breath
under junipers, grass, my face in the dirt, hiding from the dog
claws out and the teeth, the teeth. I look into windows
to the green room where I imagine he will
tie me with a rope, like a dog to a tree. I hear the cop
sirens, the ambulance and the sound of the tow truck.

I woke up. I dreamed that I lost my binoculars.
I dreamed I had nine children. I dreamed of lists. Nine.
Eight of that, seven of the most, six of the least, five of the worst,
four of the rest. See. Look, he is here. He is in the bedroom panting.
I hear the snapping sound of a dog's wagging tail.

TWO-STAR DAY

So, what does God do on a two-star day?
Two stars one for each breast, Canopus and Arcturus,
two stars over the ocean; two stars over the big tree
in my backyard drooping branches and sleeping nuthatches
45 minutes and two stars over the geysers of Yellowstone.

Two-star day—painting a picture, breaking your heart.
My horoscope says I will have a two-star day.
A star for navigation? A star to stand on my stage?
No stars inside the cat. No stars are in the green room
or above the garden glowing through the cloud cover.
No stars inside the tadpole. Anonymous stars in the astral
plane pull me into fates, people counting cards
and measuring their money.

A crowded sky full of clouds with stars of the poor,
stars for the hungry, less two stars with an asteroid coming.
The earth rotates. I turn my head. I turn to the right.
I turn to the left. I turn.

THE DAY WAS FOUND

And the sun stood still, and the moon stayed until
the people had avenged themselves upon their enemies.

JOSHUA 10:13

I.

The day is found. It was returned to us and the gospel was revealed
in a hard wind filled with dust, bones, pollen and hair.

II.

The moon dust glazes over our eyes as it is struck by the sun.
The rain comes from the west, virga showing her skirt, pushing us
like small grains of sand. The sadness is like the grit
in the bottom of the bottle of wine—settled but lingering with bitterness.

III.

Who will be present for this journey? Who will go with me into the echoing
 canyon?
Who will stand with me in my own light? Who will lean with me into the
 dark,
while I cover my eyes with the blankets of sorrow?

IV.

The rules of my tribe are vague.
Hold onto the earth so it will maintain its tilt.
Throw things into the river, rocks, sticks,
Gaze often at the sky so as to assure yourself
the sun is not standing still.
Smile at strangers.

V.

Our eyes are prevented from seeing God.
The chosen path, singled out, deliberate,
removed.

VI.

Amazon of joy, island of depression,
Cyprus, the navigational pull controlling the human path
down the arm, the gap between brain and planet that is the hand,
moon and stars of deep grief, stroke damaged abyss,
the grand canyon of tumor, gunfire to 25,000 genes in the brain,
100 billion neurons.

VII.

Trial by ordeal.
Not dead but lost.

VIII.

For someone, today will be the end of the world.
For someone today, it is the end of the world.

IX.

The sun is a clock. I am standing in my own light.
Cats are not clocks. They sit. Close, open, close, open, close their eyes.
The day is now. Today was the exact day. The day of cosmos and sunflowers.
The day returned to me.

LOVE IN A DRAWER

I love you even though you have been gone years.
Tiny fragments of paper float around my house, ringing
small bells of recognition like messages in pillowcase,
slipped into a manila file, placed carefully under magnets
notes above the sink, stored in the email, in my phone.
I can no longer leave notes on your counter
so I float messages in a bottle, freeze text an ice cube, stir my
heart into the sugar bowl, tape messages to the steering wheel,
under the wiper, write on mirror.

RUBY THROAT AND THE SWORD SWALLOWER: A TRUE STORY

Think of a day crowded with the emptiness of cat-less-ness.
The cat did not die resting under a juniper alone. He is saved.

The underside of tragedy is roughed up, but redeemed,
the part where people survive bear attack, an Airedale rescues
a drowning baby, or in this case, the soft white cat swallowed
a hummingbird whole, beak and all, while hunting
under the bleeding heart. He is saved

by a quick Heimlich maneuver. I am left holding the needle-like beak, head,
brain stem in a clot of blood. The lucky cat comes home as if he has not
    been pierced
by Ruby Throated, or wasted one of nine on such small prey.

AFTER A HOUSE A'FIRE

Darkness
inside of a crow,
inside of a suitcase
stashed in a closet
a plain envelope
sealed with seeds
entered like a womb,
languid liquid,
stiffness of honey in the cold,
Four p.m. coming in over
my right shoulder
sits down beside me
and holds my hand
comforts my mind and sketches
a strange story on the window
pain in condensation
forgeries of snow and ice
making that terrible banging
telling his story
coming to earth until something
has changed
the shady side of the tree,
the north side of the house
the west side of the tree
the softest side of the cat
the impatient side of the man.
Nothin' doin'
no movement,
no change
no gravity
no grace
just waiting for a cross
wind, laughing
black dog of doubt

You're early, you're late,
you're dead.
Darkness is next to me
making faces, the door closes
the moment lost.

DON'T THROW THAT LETTER AWAY—
IT CONTAINS MY ONLY ORIGINAL THOUGHT.

So, I came back to the house where there is even less than nothing going on
that couldn't be solved with a little bleach, house paint, a house fire,
a new washing machine, a crisp apple or a good idea.
Once, I wanted the dawn to burn away the house
where I came back after you threw away the letter.
I sit under the apple tree. Perhaps it has bloomed already.
Perhaps it will bloom after I leave. Perhaps I will
eat an apple, crack its crisp red skin.
I knew how to paint, to bleach, to wash, to bake,
to wash apples and to do even less than nothing.

The pastor says there is no original thought.
Eve says, Take a chance. She almost remembers his name.
She did not burn the house down. Restraint does not prevent evil
or indulgence. It holds her back, from fertility, grace.
Write this down. *God gave us imaginations.*
We all seek. We launder our ideas.
We filter the sand, smells, blood, stains
into art and words worth reading.

Eggs lie in nests waiting to be hatched.
Ideas rest in minds waiting to be released.
Inspiration comes like deer, gently walking,
into the yard to eat crisp red apples to give us
one more original thought.

Free. Open. Amen.

www.ingramcontent.com/pod-product-compliance
Lightning Source LLC
Chambersburg PA
CBHW061512040426
42450CB00008B/1586